WORLD ALMANAC® LIBRARY OF THE MIDDLE AGES

monarchs

FIONA MACDONALD

WORLD ALMANAC® LIBRARY

Please visit our web site at: www.worldalmanaclibrary.com
For a free color catalog describing World Almanac® Library's list of high-quality books
and multimedia programs, call 1-800-848-2928 (USA) or 1-800-387-3178 (Canada).
World Almanac® Library's fax: (414) 332-3567.

Library of Congress Cataloging-in-Publication Data

Macdonald, Fiona.
      Monarchs in the Middle Ages / by Fiona Macdonald.
          p. cm. — (World Almanac Library of the Middle Ages)
      Includes bibliographical references and index.
      ISBN 0-8368-5896-4 (lib. bdg.)
      ISBN 0-8368-5905-7 (softcover)
      1. Europe—Politics and government—476-1492—Juvenile literature.   2. Middle Ages—
   History—Juvenile literature.   3. Europe—History—476-1492—Juvenile literature.
   4. Monarchy—Europe—History—Juvenile literature.   I. Title.   II. Series.
   D131.M27   2005
   940.1—dc22   2005043263

First published in 2006 by
World Almanac® Library
A Member of the WRC Media Family of Companies
330 West Olive Street, Suite 100
Milwaukee, WI 53212 USA

Copyright © 2006 by World Almanac® Library.

Produced by White-Thomson Publishing Ltd.
Editor: Walter Kossmann
Volume editor: Peg Goldstein
Designer: Malcolm Walker
Photo researcher: Amy Sparks
World Almanac® Library editorial direction: Valerie J. Weber
World Almanac® Library editor: Jenette Donovan Guntly
World Almanac® Library art direction: Tammy West
World Almanac® Library graphic design: Kami Koenig
World Almanac® Library production: Jessica Morris and Robert Kraus

Photo credits:
Akg-Images pp. cover and pp. 4 (Bibliothéque Nationale, France), 19 (Juergen Sorges); Art Archive
pp. 14 (Bargello Museum, Florence/Dagli Orti), 33 (Museo Correr, Venice/Dagli Orti), 35 (Topkapi Museum,
Istanbul/Dagli Orti); Bridgeman Art Library pp. title page and 8, (Arxiu de la Paeria, Lleida, Spain/Index),
5 (Bibliothéque Municipale, Castres, France/Giraudon), 7 (Chetham's Library, Manchester, UK), 9, 17, 28,
40 (British Library, London), 10, 12, 22, 29 (Bibliothéque Nationale, Paris), 13 (Bibliothéque Municipale,
Rouen, France/ Giraudon), 15 (Biblioteca Estense, Modena, Italy), 16 (Bibliothéque Municipale, Castres,
France), 18 (Fitzwilliam Museum, University of Cambridge, UK), 20 (Historiska Museet, Stockholm), 23
(Landes Bibliothek, Fulda, Germany), 24 (Great Mosque, Cordoba, Spain/Giraudon), 25 (Biblioteca
Monasterio del Escorial, Madrid/Index), 6, 26 (Musee de la Tapisserie, Bayeux, France), 27 (Dept. of the
Environment, London), 30 (Bibliothéque Municipale de Lyon, France), 31 (Louvre, Paris, Lauros/ Giraudon),
34 (San Vitale, Ravenna, Italy/Giraudon), 37 (Lambeth Palace Library, London), 38 (National Portrait
Gallery, London), 42, 43 (Palazzo Medici-Riccardi, Florence).

Cover: The French king Jean the Good and his wife, Queen Jeanne, enter a city.
Title page: A twelfth-century German artist portrayed Holy Roman Emperor Frederick I
with his two sons.

Printed in Canada

1 2 3 4 5 6 7 8 9 09 08 07 06 05

Contents

Words that appear in the glossary are printed in **boldface** type the first time they occur in the text.

Source References on page 45 give bibliographical information on quoted material. See numbers ([1]) at the bottom of quotations for their source numbers.

he Middle Ages are the period between ancient and early modern times—the years from about A.D. 500 to 1500. In that time, Europe changed dramatically. The Middle Ages began with the collapse of the **Roman Empire** and with "barbarian" tribes invading from the north and east. In the early years of the Middle Ages, western European farmers struggled to survive. This period ended with European merchants eagerly seeking new international markets, European travelers searching for lands and continents unknown to them to explore, European artists creating revolutionary new styles, and European thinkers developing powerful new ideas in religion, government, and philosophy.

What Were the "Middle Ages" Like?

Some people view the period as the "Dark Ages," an era marked by ignorance and brutality. It is true that **medieval** people faced difficult lives marred by hard work, deadly diseases, and dreadful wars, but their lives included more than that.

A HISTORIAN'S VIEW

"A hundred years ago the medieval centuries... were widely regarded as 'The Dark Ages.'... It was an age whose art was barbaric or 'Gothic'—a millennium of darkness—a thousand years without a bath. Today... scholarship [has] demonstrated clearly that the medieval period was an epoch of immense vitality and profound creativity."
C. Warren Hollister

The Middle Ages were also a time of growing population, developing technology, increasing trade, and fresh ideas. New villages and towns were built; new fields were cleared; and, with the help of new tools like the wheeled iron plow, farms produced more food. **Caravans** brought silks and spices from faraway lands in Asia. New sports and games, such as soccer, golf, chess, and playing cards, became popular. Musicians, singers, acrobats, and dancers entertained crowds at fairs and festivals. Traveling troupes performed plays that mixed humor with moral messages for anyone who would stop and listen.

Religion, education, and government all changed. Christianity spread throughout Europe and became more powerful. Another major faith—Islam—was born and carried into Europe from the Middle East. New schools and universities trained young men as scholars or for

◀ King Jean the Good of France (ruled 1350–1364) and his wife, Queen Jeanne, arrive at a city in fine style. The king is dressed in long blue robes decorated with golden fleurs-de-lis (irises, an emblem of the French monarchy).

◀ King Childeric II ruled Austrasia (now part of France and Germany) from A.D. 653 to 673. He is shown here with three symbols of kingship, which were used by most medieval monarchs to proclaim their power: a crown, a throne (raised royal seat), and a scepter (long staff).

careers in the Church, medicine, and the law. Medieval rulers, judges, and ordinary citizens created **parliaments**, jury trials, and the common law. These changes in the fabric of society still shape our world today.

Historians divide the entire period into two parts. In the early Middle Ages, from about A.D. 500 to 1000, Europe adjusted to the changes caused by the fall of the Roman Empire and the formation of new kingdoms by Germanic peoples. In these years, the Christian Church took form and Europeans withstood new invasions. In the late Middle Ages, from about 1000 to 1500, medieval life and culture matured. This period saw population growth and economic expansion, the rise of towns and universities, the building of great cathedrals and mosques, and the launching of the **Crusades**.

Who Ruled Medieval Europe?

Throughout the Middle Ages, the destiny of Europe was controlled by a few powerful men— and even fewer powerful women. These monarchs (sole rulers) were often outstanding individuals—

tough in mind and body, bold, greedy, ambitious, and strong-willed. Sometimes, they were taller, fatter, and fitter than the poorly fed ordinary people, and their faces were less blemished, and their bodies less deformed by poor nourishment, hard work, and disease. Their public appearances were carefully stage-managed to create an image of royal magnificence. Some monarchs claimed to have holy ancestry or divine protection or encouraged their subjects to think they had superhuman powers.

Medieval monarchs were known by many different names: emperor, king, queen, prince, chieftain, elector and—in southern Europe— **doge, caliph**, and emir. Some of these titles, such as king or emperor, looked back to past, glorious civilizations—especially to the Roman Empire that ruled Europe from the first century B.C. to the fifth century A.D. Others, such as prince, chief, or doge, were based on words meaning "leader" or "commander." No matter what they were called, medieval monarchs all had the same essential duties—guarding and guiding their countries and the people that they ruled.

CHAPTER 1

Royal Responsibilities

ike many rulers today, medieval kings had tremendous personal power. Their own choices, views, and tastes could shape the course of events in areas that they controlled. Power, however, also brought heavy responsibilities. One modern historian has summarized these as "war, law, and [getting] the money to pay for them." If a monarch ignored these responsibilities or failed to honor them, he or she might lose his or her throne.

War Leaders

The earliest medieval monarchs were warlords—heads of kinship groups, such as tribes or clans. In troubled times between about A.D. 500 to 1000, they kept hold of power by force. Early medieval regions controlled by rulers, such as kings, had few fixed frontiers. Their populations changed, too, as warring tribes migrated to settle in distant territory. Early medieval rulers had to be always ready to face invasion or attack. Many also aimed to conquer new lands or capture rich treasures to make themselves, and their subjects, stronger, safer, and more prosperous.

ROYAL DUTIES

"It is a merciful practice for a king to consider with prudent care the needs of . . . all people subject to him."
The Edict of Paris, 614, made by King Clothar II of the Franks [2]

▼ King Edward the Confessor of England ruled from 1042 to 1066. The year he died, his kingdom in England was invaded twice, first from Norway and then from Normandy (now in France); both wanted to rule English lands.

◀ King Stephen of England fought his cousin Matilda for the right to rule the kingdom of England. She had the better claim in law to be monarch; he had a stronger army. The year before Stephen died, he agreed to name Matilda's son Henry as the next king of England. Matilda's son ruled as Henry II from 1154 to 1189.

Later medieval monarchs were also war leaders. They had to defend their own family lands and castles from invaders, together with all the other territory they ruled. They were responsible for summoning armies, keeping them loyal, and commanding them in battle. They had to show boldness, courage, and military skill as well as inspire soldiers to follow them—even if this meant risking or losing their own lives.

Peacekeepers and Lawmakers

Throughout the Middle Ages, rulers were also peacemakers and guardians of justice. As the most powerful people in their kingdoms, they were expected to protect the poor, weak, and humble. They had to persuade all members of society to work together for the common good. It was their duty to be fair and honest, to tell the truth, and to hand out punishments and rewards without fear or favor.

Kings appointed judges and set up courts where their subjects could ask for quarrels to be settled and criminals to be condemned. They sent royal officials to maintain law and order in local communities and organized patrols to catch robbers, pirates, and highwaymen. They built prisons where criminals could be locked up. They

KINGS HAD TO BE TOUGH

"When [rivals and rebels] . . . saw that King Stephen [who ruled England 1135–1154] was a kind, pleasant and easy-going man who did not punish his enemies, then they committed all sorts of horrible crimes."
Adapted from The Anglo-Saxon Chronicle [3]

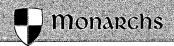

SENDING OUT LORDS OF THE REALM

"Our most serene and Christian lord and emperor, Charles, has selected the most prudent and wise from among his leading men, archbishops and bishops, together with venerable [honorable] abbots and devout laymen [ordinary people], and has sent them out into all his kingdom, and bestowed [given] through them on all his subjects the right to live in accordance with a right [good] rule of law."

Royal order issued by Emperor Charlemagne's government in France c. A.D. 802

asked for community cooperation through institutions, such as the English "hue and cry," which required all men to leave their work and chase criminals when the local sheriff sounded a loud hunting horn.

Many medieval rulers were also lawmakers. They created new laws to guard property, promote trade, encourage economic development, and protect (or sometimes limit) civil and religious rights. They demanded taxes to pay for armies and government officials.

Privileged People

Compared with ordinary people, medieval monarchs were extremely wealthy. They owned palaces, castles, hunting lodges, and vast **estates** with meadows, forests, and farms. They wore rich, costly robes of silk, velvet, **brocade**, fur, and the finest wool and linen, embroidered with real gold and silver thread. As a sign of rank, they appeared in public wearing magnificent jewelry —rings, necklaces, and crowns studded with glittering precious stones. Sometimes, they carried ancient talismans (charms), such as banners or weapons that were said to have magical powers. They were surrounded by servants (and sometimes slaves) to care for their personal comfort and all their practical needs.

Monarchs were guided by spiritual councillors; in Christian countries, these were priests, monks,

▲ King James II the Just of Spain meets with members of a parliament (assembly of local representatives and royal councillors) in the city of Barcelona in 1311.

and scholars trained by the Church. They were advised—and sometimes tricked or bullied—by councillors, bankers, lawyers, accountants, and politicians. In addition, monarchs were guarded almost constantly by warriors—**knights** and foot soldiers—who also fought alongside them during wartime.

The Right to Rule

How did medieval monarchs justify so many privileges and so much special attention? Some claimed the right to rule through their physical prowess and strength of will. They were strong, tough, clever, cunning, or brutal. By winning control over their fellow men and women or earning their confidence, they also won power to rule. Powerful nobles chose other rulers. Some inherited power from their fathers, brothers, grandfathers, uncles, and even, in some cases, their mothers.

Before about A.D. 1000 (or later, in parts of eastern Europe), **inheritance** laws were not firmly fixed. Many early medieval monarchs had to fight for the right to rule. They had to defeat challenges from their own family members as well as other ambitious men. All the sons of a monarch—and other close male relatives—might try to claim his throne. Often, there were many claimants, since early medieval monarchs married several times and also usually had many other sexual partners who bore them sons. Royal women schemed and even murdered to help their sons come to power. Royal sons also ganged up against each other or looked for powerful allies to help them become king.

Chosen Heirs

Some royal fathers tried to keep wars from wrecking their kingdoms by choosing just one son to succeed (follow them as king). To further strengthen their son's claim, they announced this choice by royal proclamation or in public ceremonies. Sometimes, they appointed guardians and regents to watch over their kingdom and support their chosen heir. Some rulers, such as Christian emperor Charlemagne, followed ancient Germanic customs and divided their lands among several sons. This division

prevented disputes, but the new states it created were smaller and weaker than the old undivided kingdom had been.

Throughout the centuries, many countries developed new laws that governed the right of sons to inherit kingdoms from their fathers. These laws were not all the same, but in many parts of Europe, including the strongest, richest kingdoms, such as England and France, they gave the oldest son the right to inherit all his father's land. (This was called primogeniture.)

If there were no sons, royal land might pass to a brother or nephew or be divided among a ruler's daughters. As soon as they married, though, the land passed to their husbands, who then claimed the right to rule it. This was a quick—and peaceful—way of enlarging a kingdom. The rulers of medieval Austria were famous for their skill at arranging marriage alliances. They boasted, "Other states make war, but fortunate Austria gets married!"

Pleasing the People

Medieval monarchs had strong supporters—knights, nobles, and sometimes, clergy—who helped them rule and shared in their wealth and privileges. It was impossible, though, for rulers to force all their subjects to obey them. They, therefore, tried to win public support and approval. They held royal audiences (meetings) and made progresses (stately journeys) around their kingdoms to listen to complaints or appointed special commissioners (representatives) to do this on their behalf.

△ King Henry II of England (*center*) ruled from 1154 to 1189. Here, he serves his young son Henry (*far right*) with a cup of wine during a ceremony held in 1170 to nominate young Henry as the future king of England. In fact, young Henry died before his father, and his brother, Richard I, became the next king.

AN ENGLISH SCHOLAR DESCRIBES KINGS

"Kings are like God to their subjects. So great is the majesty of this Earth's highest, that people never weary of looking at them, and those that live with them are looked on as being above the rest of mankind. No wonder crowds of women and children rush to gaze at them, so do grown men."
Henry of Huntingdon, twelfth century [5]

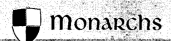
► Popes also called on medieval monarchs to take action to defend the Christian Church and Christian people. This medieval **manuscript** shows Pope Urban II preaching a powerful sermon in 1095, asking Christian monarchs to fight against Muslims in the Middle East.

Monarchs also met representatives of local communities, whom they summoned (called by law) to attend councils and parliaments. These meetings became increasingly important after about 1250. Members of parliaments began to criticize royal policy and demand the right to be consulted on new laws and new taxes.

Church and State

In A.D. 500, Christians lived in most parts of the old Roman Empire, which were lands formerly ruled by Rome but abandoned between about A.D. 350 to 500. The lands stretched from today's Germany to North Africa and the Middle East. Many people living in these lands were still **pagans**, however. Most pagan peoples believed that their ruler had a special relationship with the gods or even that rulers shared the gods'

magic powers. This probably gave the kings extra confidence and helped persuade people to follow them. Throughout the years, though, Christian missionaries managed to convert almost all Europe's rulers, and these rulers forced their subjects to follow the Christian faith.

Christians also believed that kings were special and sacred. Medieval writers called them "part man, part God." Like Jesus Christ, kings had to be prepared to suffer to save their people. Like priests, they were meant to serve them. With good leadership, kings could help their subjects live better, more devout lives. The Church taught that rulers were chosen by God, who gave them a **divine right** to rule. This was symbolized in **coronation** services—where monarchs promised to serve their country and were blessed by priests with chrism (holy oil). It was a religious duty to obey a crowned king; to rebel against one was an insult to God.

In southern Europe (present-day Spain, Portugal, southern Italy, and Sicily), there were Muslim rulers and multifaith communities from about A.D. 800 and onward. Muslim monarchs in Europe were known as emirs (princes) or caliphs—an Arabic word that meant "deputies" or "successors" to the prophet Muhammad.

GOD AND EMPERORS

"God sets Emperors on the throne and gives them lordship over all."
Constantine VII, emperor of **Byzantium** 913–953 [6]

(Caliphs also ruled in Muslim lands in North Africa and the Middle East.) Like Christian monarchs elsewhere in Europe, Muslim rulers had religious responsibilities. Their duty was to lead the Muslim community in spiritual and worldly matters, encourage the spread of Islam, and uphold Muslim holy law.

Church Power

Religious teachings greatly strengthened medieval rulers' prestige. In return, leaders of the Christian Church asked Christian monarchs for protection against enemies. This did not, however, stop them from quarreling with monarchs whose policies conflicted with the Church's religious or political aims.

In western Europe, popes based in Rome led the Church. Their chief task was to care for the spiritual welfare of Christian people. Popes were also landowners. They ruled the Papal States, a group of small states in central Italy, and controlled a large, well-trained staff of church lawyers and administrators. Popes, mostly chosen from powerful noble families, often took part in international politics. Few monarchs dared anger or contradict them. If they did, they might be **excommunicated**. Their lands would be placed under an **interdict**—no one living there would be allowed to get married, inherit land, be baptized, or be buried with religious ceremonies.

Why No Women?

There were very few women rulers in the Middle Ages for three main reasons. First, only male warriors or tribal leaders were thought capable of ruling a country. Women's tasks were to bear children; care for their home, husband, and family; and protect the homes and families while men were away. Second, the laws of most European countries treated women like children—unable to take part in most important activities open to men. In pre-Christian times (until about A.D. 600 in Britain but until 1200 in Baltic lands, including Estonia, Latvia, and Finland), women in northern Europe could own

BYZANTINE EMPEROR ALEXIUS I COMNENUS (RULED 1081–1118)

"The emperor was prepared to face wars against the barbarians, with all their troubles and dangers, but he preferred to leave the running of government business, the choice of judges, and the accounts of empire finances to his mother. . . . [She] had an exceptional understanding of businesses and politics, a genius for organization and government; in fact, she was capable of managing not only the Byzantine Empire, but any other empire, as well."
Byzantine princess Anna Comnena writing in the 1140s describes her father, the emperor, and her grandmother [7]

land and property, take legal action, and even get divorced. In southern Europe and elsewhere after Christianity became accepted, however, laws prevented most women from owning land, getting an education, or serving as a judge, juror, or witness in court. Third, the Christian Church taught that women were untrustworthy by nature and unfit for government.

In spite of this, some medieval women—the wives, mothers, and daughters of monarchs—played an important part in medieval government. They acted as diplomats, hostesses, advisers, guardians, and peacemakers.

Women with Power

Some royal women became powerful by persuading men to do what they wanted. Others acted as deputies while their husbands were away. A few exceptional women took power themselves. For example, Queen Blanche of France (lived 1188–1252) was married at age twelve to King Louis VIII. As she grew older, she helped him by discussing war campaigns and government plans. When King Louis died, leaving their young son to inherit the throne, Queen Blanche ruled France for about eight years, until the boy was old enough to take control. Even after this, Queen Blanche continued to advise him. She also ran the country while he was

► Queen Blanche of France (*left*) supervises the education of her son, the young King Louis IX. A schoolmaster (*right*) is ready to beat the young king if he forgets his lessons. Louis was later made a saint by the Catholic Church. The artist has therefore shown him with a halo—a sign of sainthood.

fighting the Crusades in foreign lands. She arranged peace treaties to increase the French monarchy's power and married her children to heirs and heiresses who possessed vast estates of land. With each wedding, more of France came under the control of the French royal family. When French nobles rebelled against Queen Blanche's rule, she led an army to fight them, riding on a white horse. In 1229, she defeated Count Raymond of Toulouse, who controlled vast estates in Languedoc, an independent region of southwest France. This was an important step toward absorbing Languedoc into the French kingdom.

Royal Image and Reality

A king's royal **status** and his wealth and power affected the way he was seen in public. He was usually kept separate from ordinary people or displayed high above them on a throne. He wore

PEACE-KEEPING QUEEN

*"By her advice peace wraps the kingdom round
And keeps mankind from breaking acts of peace."*
Praise of Queen Edith, wife of Anglo-Saxon King Edward the Confessor (ruled 1042–1066)

a jeweled crown (symbol of the sun—"king" of the heavens) and held royal symbols such as an upright sword, representing justice, or an orb and scepter (globe and staff). Both were signs of worldly power.

Their high status and concern for their public image also shaped the way kings were portrayed. Few lifelike pictures of medieval rulers were made. Instead, artists created icons (ideal images in paint or stone) that made monarchs look superhuman. Kings were pictured as manly, strong, and handsome. Queens were beautiful, gentle, and wise. Sometimes, a ruler's image was made from rare and costly materials, such as gold, marble, or semiprecious stones, to stress the difference between monarchs and ordinary people.

Medieval kings also used art as a way of advertising their achievements and recording important events during their reigns. They paid for scribes to write royal **chronicles** (lists of important events) or make collections of royal laws. These might be decorated with pictures of the king and his council. Manuscript illustrations showed kings and queens making gifts to churches and monasteries. Sometimes—to remind viewers of royalty's half-holy status—they were shown standing next to saints or angels, who offer them guidance and protection.

◁ Nobles could not sit down in the presence of a king unless he invited them to do so. Ordinary people had to kneel. Here, the scholar Jean de Meung (lived 1240–1305) kneels as he presents a copy of his latest book to King Philip the Handsome of France.

Royal Memorials

Most medieval rulers wanted to make sure that they were remembered after they died, so they commissioned artists to create memorial statues to be placed above their tombs or in fine buildings, such as cathedrals, that they had funded. These statues show kings dressed in magnificent armor and queens wearing rich robes and crowns. Royal tombs were also decorated with each king's emblem (personal symbol) or **coat of arms**.

Eleanor Crosses

King Edward I of England was devoted to his wife, Eleanor of Castile. When she died in 1290 in the city of Lincoln, he gave orders for her body to be carried to London for burial. He paid for twelve beautiful stone crosses to be carved and had one placed at each spot where her coffin had rested overnight on its journey. The district of Charing Cross in London is still named after one of these crosses today.

the age of migrations

The early years of the Middle Ages, from around A.D. 500 to 1000, were a time of great upheaval. New peoples came to live in Europe, and new monarchs seized power. Old, powerful empires collapsed, and many new, smaller kingdoms were created. Old art, architecture, books, and manuscripts were temporarily lost—or, sometimes, destroyed forever. "Civilized" traditions were challenged, and for a while, it looked as if unfamiliar new customs would replace them. Medieval people called these customs "barbaric." Due to this, the early medieval era is sometimes called "the Dark Ages," or "the Age of Migrations."

Roman Heritage

From 27 B.C. until A.D. 476, Roman emperors ruled much of Europe, North Africa, and the Middle East. They commanded armies, appointed judges and provincial (regional) governors, levied new taxes, and helped shape new laws. They issued coins decorated with their portraits, paid for splendid public monuments, and were the chief priests of the state religion. After they died, many of them were honored as gods. All these Roman emperors lived before the Middle Ages began. Their names and deeds were not forgotten, however, and many medieval monarchs tried to copy the way they ruled. Some even took Roman names, such as Philip II Augustus who ruled France from 1180 to 1223.

In A.D. 395, the Roman Empire was divided. Emperors based in Rome ruled western Europe; Roman lands in eastern Europe and the Middle East were ruled from a new capital city, Constantinople (now Istanbul, Turkey). At first, the emperors there continued Roman traditions of government, but these were soon altered by new ideas about kingship taken from the Christian faith and also from Middle Eastern customs. The eastern emperors became known by a new name, the Byzantines.

"Barbarian" Attacks

In western Europe, Roman rule was disrupted as groups of migrating people moved to settle in new lands. For example, from about 300, the **Franks**, originally from present-day Germany, migrated to live in northern France. Then, after about 370, the old Roman Empire lands—east and west—were attacked by hostile tribes: Huns, Goths, Alans, Visigoths, and Vandals. The Huns, led by their king, Attila, came from Central Asia. Other tribes migrated from northern and eastern Europe. The Romans called them all "barbarians," saying they were brutal and uncivilized.

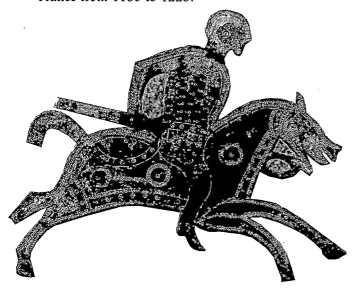

◄ This bronze plaque (carved slab), made about A.D. 600, shows a barbarian horseman riding to attack. He wears body armor of small metal plates fastened to a leather jerkin (sleeveless jacket) and carries a long sword in his right hand.

▲ Attila the Hun and his army are pictured in a late-medieval manuscript. The artist has shown the invading Huns' sturdy warhorses, pointed metal helmets, and long sharp spears.

Some barbarian raiders—mostly Huns—rode away from Roman lands loaded with rich booty. The Alans were defeated by Roman army generals, helped by the Franks. Although many retreated, some stragglers settled. Many Goths, Visigoths, and Vandals also conquered land and settled on it. They founded new kingdoms in present-day Spain, Italy, North Africa, and southern France.

New rulers, such as Theodoric the Great (king of the Ostrogoths, the eastern Goths, 471–526), took over old Roman lands and doled them out among their followers. At first, settlers and local people were ruled according to their own systems of law. They were also forbidden to marry outside their own group. Warlike barbarian kings continued to wear traditional robes and hairstyles and magnificent jewelry. All were very different from sober Roman styles. To many people, these traditions were a sign of savagery. Soon, however, the separate Roman and barbarian cultures began to blend together. Barbarian kings became Christians. They employed former Roman officials—trained under the old Roman Empire—to manage their kingdoms. Their laws were translated into Latin, the language of the Roman Empire and the Christian Church.

Attila the Hun
(ruled a.d. 434–453)

Called the "Scourge [cruel whip] of God," Attila, king of the Huns, was the most famous barbarian invader to attack Rome. From his base in what is now Hungary, he fought across a vast territory from today's eastern Germany to Central Asia. He conquered the eastern half of the Roman Empire and then, from 451 to 452, invaded France and Italy. He threatened to destroy the splendid city of Rome but was bought off with gold and treasure by Pope Leo I. After Attila died, the Huns lost power, but their attacks seriously damaged the old, weak Roman Empire and encouraged other invaders who soon followed them.

In 476, after more than one hundred years of invasions, the western Roman Empire collapsed, and the last Roman emperor was forced to flee from Rome. He was replaced by a Germanic warlord, Odoacer, who became king. Nevertheless, barbarian invasions continued. For example, in 568, **Lombard** ("Long-beard") raiders from Germany conquered northern Italy. They set up a new kingdom based in Milan. It survived for more than two hundred years before being conquered by the Franks.

A New Roman Empire?

While Roman power was collapsing, powerful leaders in many parts of northern Europe seized their chance to set up their own new kingdoms.

By far the most successful was Charlemagne ("Charles the Great," ruled A.D. 768–814), king of the Franks, a group of farmers and soldiers who lived in southern Germany and northern France.

Charlemagne was descended from a famous family. His grandfather, Charles Martel the Hammer who ruled the whole Frankish kingdom from 719 to 741, was not royal by birth. In 732, however, he defeated an invading Muslim army and prevented northern Europe from becoming part of the Muslim empire. Martel's son, Pepin the Short (ruled 751–768), saved the pope from Lombard attack. Pepin left his kingdom to both his sons to rule jointly. After three years, one son died. The survivor, Charlemagne, ruled alone.

During Charlemagne's rule, the Franks became very powerful. They conquered the Lombards in Italy and pagan tribes in Germany. Charlemagne appointed counts (trusted noblemen) to administer justice throughout his empire and sent officials with written instructions (unknown

since Roman times) to carry out his commands. To loyal noble warriors, he gave large areas of conquered land together with the peasant farmers who lived there. In return, he ordered the nobles to come and fight for him, bringing well-trained soldiers (knights) with them.

RESULTS OF THE LOMBARD INVASIONS

"Everywhere, we see war, and hear moans and cries. Our cities are wrecked, our fortresses are crushed, our land is devastated. No-one is left to plough the fields or protect the towns."
Pope Gregory I, c. 600

Charlemagne

King Charlemagne was a large man, 6 feet, 4 inches (1.9 meters), tall and broadly built. He spoke quietly but was cheerful and talkative and enjoyed debating. He drank only a little but ate a great deal. He hated wearing fine silk clothes and preferred a shirt, tunic, and tight leggings, in Frankish style, together with a blue wool cloak and a sword with a gold and silver hilt (handle). In the winter, he wore a cloak of otter or rat skins. He loved riding, hunting, swimming, and pretty women. He was married several times according to Church laws and also had extra wives according to Frankish customs, plus four concubines (unofficial extra wives). He understood Latin (the language of scholars) and could probably read it, but he could not write.
Based on *Life of Charlemagne*, written by Einhard, a monk, c. 820

◀ Charlemagne, king of the Franks, is crowned Holy Roman Emperor by Pope Leo III in A.D. 800. Charlemagne kneels in prayer before the pope as a sign that he wishes to rule as a Christian king and will follow the moral and spiritual guidance of the Christian Church.

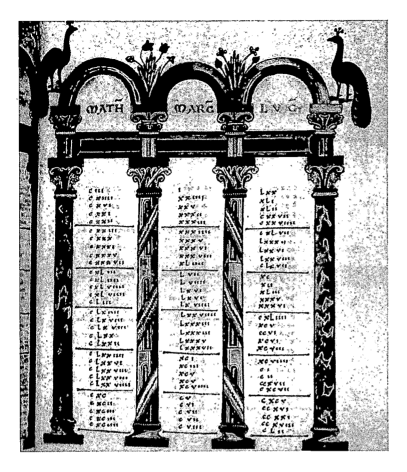

◀ Charlemagne's scholars produced many fine manuscripts, like this collection of Christian Church laws written and decorated around A.D. 800. They used handwriting and decorative patterns based on styles popular in ancient Rome over three hundred years before Charlemagne came to power. This style fit in with Charlemagne's goal to rule lands that once belonged to the old Roman Empire.

Charlemagne brutally forced all the people he conquered to convert to Christianity, but he had a gentler side to his character. He admired art and literature and invited the best scholars in Europe to live and work at his court. He built a splendid palace (with a library, chapel, school— and even a swimming pool) at Aachen/Aix-la-Chapelle, on the borders of today's Germany and France. On Christmas Day 800, Pope Leo III crowned Charlemagne "Holy Roman Emperor." Leo hoped to create a new Christian kingdom to rule Europe, replacing the old Roman Empire. After Charlemagne died, however, the empire did not survive for long.

The Seven Kingdoms of England
England had once been part of the Roman Empire, but the last Roman soldiers left in 409. After this, the people of Britain were ruled by local kings. Some spoke Latin (the Roman language) and lived in Roman style in large, comfortable villas (grand country houses) with baths, gardens, central heating, and beautiful **mosaic** floors. Others, in the far north and west (modern Scotland, Ireland, and Wales) where **Celtic** civilization existed, were warriors, raiders, and warlords. Their power came from their physical strength and mental toughness and from their armies of loyal fighting men.

Once the Romans left, Britain's farmland was a tempting target for foreign invaders. By about 600, thousands of settler families had arrived: **Saxons** from lands now known as Germany, **Angles** and Jutes from present-day Denmark, and Frisians from the area of modern Netherlands. (Today, they are often all called "Anglo-Saxons.") Their leaders fought each other—and British people—for the right to rule, and by about 700, Anglo-Saxon warlords controlled all England. By 800, they had set up seven strong kingdoms:

Northumbria in the north, Mercia in central England, East Anglia and Essex in the east, Kent and Sussex in the far southeast, and Wessex in the southwest.

The Anglo-Saxon kingdoms were often at war. Their power depended on their rulers—each one wanted to become Bretwalda (Lord of Britain). During the reign of King Offa (757–796), Mercia became the strongest kingdom. Offa built a huge earth wall called Offa's Dyke to defend his kingdom from an attack from Wales. He also minted the first English silver coins, bearing his portrait in Roman style.

Beginning in 878, Wessex, ruled by King Alfred the Great, became stronger. That year, Alfred forced **Viking** armies that had invaded from Scandinavia to agree to a peace treaty. For the next two hundred years, Vikings ruled north-eastern England. This area became known as the

LETTER FROM KING ALFRED

"To me it seems right and good . . . that we should . . . translate those [Christian] books that are vitally important for all people to know into a language we can all understand."
Adapted by author

Danelaw; Viking rule lasted there until 954.

Like Charlemagne, Alfred was a Christian king who valued art and learning. He built new towns and churches throughout his kingdom, strengthened defense, and promoted trade. He encouraged scholars to spread Christianity and to prepare English translations of important Christian books. He was the first king in England known to be able to read and write.

Celtic Borders

While Anglo-Saxon kings controlled the south and west of Britain (most of modern-day England), Celtic warlords ruled kingdoms in lands known today as Scotland, Ireland, and

▼ This silver penny, made during King Offa's reign, is over twelve hundred years old. On one side, a portrait of King Offa, surrounded by the words "OFFA REX" (Offa the King) is still clearly visible. Besides being used as money, coins also advertised the power of the kings who commanded that they were made.

GReat Anglo-Saxon kings

- Athelstan (ruled 924–939): The first king to rule all England; he united the Seven Kingdoms and led English armies to victory against soldiers in Scotland.
- Ethelred II (ruled 978–1016): Tried to buy peace from Viking invaders by offering them **Danegeld**. Each time he paid them, however, they came back for more money.
- Edward the Confessor (ruled 1042–1066): Peaceful and pious, Edward built the first church where Westminster Abbey in London now stands.

▽ Viking warriors on board a Viking warship are portrayed on a picture stone made in Jutland (now Denmark) around A.D. 850. Each warrior vowed loyalty to his local warlord. The strongest Viking warlords eventually defeated their rivals and became kings.

Wales. They were descended from peoples who had lived in western Europe for thousands of years, long before the Romans invaded Britain.

All three of these lands were divided among different peoples, but the Celtic warrior-kings wanted to unite each of them. For example, in 843, Celtic monarch Kenneth MacAlpine joined the two largest states in Scotland, Dalriada in the northwest and Pict-land in the northeast, into one united kingdom. By 1018, its kings had taken control of most of Scotland. In Wales, Rhodri Mawr, king of the region of Gwynndd from 844 to 887, became the first man to rule the whole country after marrying a princess from the second-strongest region, Ceredigion. In Ireland, the most powerful rulers became High Kings; for example, Brian Boru ruled the district of Munster from 976 to 1014 and fought against Viking invaders.

Viking Attacks and Rule

Beginning in about 800, Viking raiders sailed from Norway, Denmark, and Sweden to attack rich monasteries and trading centers throughout Europe. Viking merchants traveled as far as the Middle East to seek peaceful trade. Viking families left their homes to find land and to escape control by increasingly powerful kings. They settled in Iceland, Greenland, England, Scotland, Ireland, and northern France. Viking explorers also sailed to North America, landing in Newfoundland about 1000.

Traditionally, Viking people had two systems of government: loyalty to local chieftains and village democracy. Viking villagers prized justice, fairness, and free speech. They held the world's first parliaments, local assemblies called "Things," where villagers met to punish wrong-doers and make new laws. Viking chieftains became more powerful by raiding and conquering foreign lands. By about 1000, Norway, Denmark, and Sweden were all ruled by strong kings, and

Vikings in Paris

In March 845, 120 Viking ships sailed up the Seine River to Paris, wrecking everything. Charles the Bald (ruled 843–877), king of the Frankish people who lived there, tried to defend the city but soon realized that his armies could not possibly defeat the invaders. So he made a deal with the Vikings. He gave them 7,000 pounds (3,175 kilograms) of silver, as a payment for ending their attack. This stopped them from advancing and persuaded them to go away.
Adapted from *Annals (history) of St. Bertin*, written by a French monk, 845

▼ This is a modern reconstruction of a Viking farm built about 1000 at L'Anse aux Meadows, Newfoundland, Canada. Viking farmers and their families in Europe would have lived in the wooden farmhouse (*back*) with its turf-covered roof and wooden walls.

Strong Viking Rulers

- Guthrum—Set up Viking kingdom (Danelaw) in north and east England.
- Erik Bloodaxe—Killed seven of his brothers so that he could become king of Norway in the 930s. Last Viking ruler of northeast England. Forced to flee by enemies in 954.
- Harald Bluetooth—King of Denmark. Converted Danish Vikings to Christianity about 960. Built splendid monuments, also Scandinavia's first bridge.
- Svein Forkbeard—Ruled Denmark 998–1014. Led many Viking raids, then invaded England in 1013. Died five weeks later.
- Harald Hardrada—King of Norway, led Viking army to invade England in 1066; he died in battle.
- Sihtric Silkbeard—Ruled Viking kingdom based in Dublin, Ireland, from 989–1036. Fought against Irish kings.
- Thorfinn the Mighty—Ruled Orkney Islands off Scotland, 1020–1056, and defeated attacks from Scottish kings.

local assemblies were much less important. The most powerful Viking king, Canute the Great (ruled 1016–1035), controlled an empire that included Denmark, Norway, and large parts of the British Isles.

Viking raids across Europe ended soon after 1100, but Viking settlements, languages, and traditions remained. Lands where the Vikings settled in northern France became the powerful **Duchy** of Normandy. Scandinavian kings ruled Orkney, Shetland, and other islands close to Scotland until 1469.

Russian Kingdoms

Vikings also traveled east across the Baltic Sea and into Russia, where they built forts and trading settlements. The largest was at Kiev, now in present-day Ukraine. According to Russian chronicles, a Viking warrior, Rurik, became the first Russian king. He was chosen by the Slav people in about 860. They wanted a strong leader to end fighting among their tribes. The chronicles tell how Rurik became ruler of Novgorod, an important trading city, then took control of northwestern Russia. His kinsman, Oleg, followed him as king, then Rurik's young son, Igor, took control. Today, historians think that Igor (ruled about 913–945) was a real person, but that Rurik and Oleg were invented later to explain the origins of the Russian royal family.

In 998, Russian prince Vladimir became a Christian and married a Byzantine princess. He made his capital, Kiev, into a splendid city. Yaroslav the Wise, king of Kiev from 1019 to 1054, sent friendly ambassadors to other European rulers, built many churches, and encouraged the first Russian literature. Scribes wrote in Cyrillic script, based on the Greek alphabet. It was introduced to Russia by Byzantine missionaries Saint Methodius and Saint Cyril who invented the alphabet.

how Russia Got Its name

The name of the modern nation Russia originates from "Rus"—the name given to Swedish Viking settlers by local Slav peoples.

Magyars in Hungary

In about 896, **Magyars** (nomads from southern Russia) were defeated by rival tribes, the Pechenegs from Turkey. Led by the warrior Prince Arpad (died around 907), the Magyars migrated west and settled in what is now Hungary. In 995, Arpad's great-great grandson, Stephen, married a German princess and became a Christian. Two years later, he was crowned Hungary's first king. He made new laws to unite the Magyar people and converted them to Christianity. After he died in 1038, he was made a saint.

CHAPTER 3

Building kingdoms

After the Viking and Magyar invasions, the age of migrations ended. Although there were still wars fought for land throughout Europe, many new, settled kingdoms had been created. The strongest were in today's England and France. Modern-day Germany and Italy, however, were still divided into small separate states, each with independent customs and laws. Their rulers struggled against each other, trying to win power.

Holy Roman Emperors

In Germany, Henry of Saxony (ruled 919–936) conquered many other German states, plus land in Hungary and Denmark. He claimed the title "King of the Germans" for his family. In 955, his son, Otto I the Great (ruled 936–973), defeated the Magyars and became even more powerful.

Since Charlemagne, rulers in France and Germany had called themselves emperors, but they did not rule Charlemagne's lands. Otto was different. He conquered Charlemagne's old empire in Switzerland and Italy. Then, in 962, he traveled to Rome, where he was crowned emperor by the pope.

For almost the next one thousand years, until 1806, German princes followed Otto as emperors and tried to increase the empire's power.

Frederick I Barbarossa ("Red Beard," ruled 1152–1190) added the words "Holy Roman" to the emperor's title and brought the princes of Poland, Hungary, and Burgundy (now Belgium, Luxembourg, and eastern France) under the empire's control. His grandson, Frederick II the

OTTO GAINS A CROWN

"Otto traveled to Rome dressed in splendid new robes and jewels; he was greeted by Pope John and blessed with holy oil. His rule of the Holy Roman Empire was also blessed by the Pope. In return, Otto gave back to the Pope the papal lands (land ruled by popes) that his armies had conquered, and he showered the Pope with rich gifts of gold, silver and precious stones."
Adapted from: Chronicle of Otto the Great, by Liudprand of Cremona

◀ King Otto I the Great (*seated*) receives homage (a promise of loyalty) from a defeated enemy, Berenger II, who ruled land in southern Italy. Berenger's warriors (*far left*) also offer homage. At the right of the picture, a member of Otto's court, backed by armored knights, proudly carries his sword.

◁ Emperor Frederick I Barbarossa (*center*) is portrayed with his two sons. All look strong, proud, and confident; all wear rich robes and jeweled crowns. Frederick's oldest son (*left*) is shown with his hand raised, giving his father wise advice.

Wonder of the World, (ruled 1220–1250) fought for years to conquer land in Italy and Sicily and to win support from powerful German Church leaders. He led the Sixth Crusade and became king of the Crusader state of Jerusalem.

Sons usually followed their fathers as Holy Roman Emperors. For example, members of the powerful Hohenstaufen family were emperors from 1138 to 1254. In law, however, emperors did not inherit the right to rule. They were chosen by leading German princes and Christian Church officials—though few of them had the power to refuse a strong family's claim.

CHOOSING A RULER

"*The most powerful men met together . . . to choose a leader . . . this is the most important part of the laws of the Holy Roman Empire. . . . Kings do not rule because of birth or family inheritance, but because they are chosen by other princes . . . At last, Frederick, duke of Swabia, son of Duke Frederick, was elected by all the other princes. Preferred by all, he was raised to the rank of king.*"
Based on *Deeds of Frederick Barbarossa* by Otto of Freising

Popes with Power

For hundreds of years, emperors quarreled bitterly with the popes in Rome. Emperors demanded the right to appoint Church leaders, but popes would not agree. If a pope refused to crown an emperor, then the emperor did not have full rights to rule. After one fierce dispute in 1077, Pope Gregory VII left Emperor Henry IV standing for three nights barefoot in the snow to ask forgiveness. Popes were helped by the powerful Welf family from Germany, who was a great enemy of the Hohenstaufen dynasty. This led to bloody **feuds** between supporters of both families that continued long after 1266, when the last Hohenstaufen ruler was killed.

Multicultural Muslim Spain

Like Germany, the area now known as Spain also had many rulers. In the far north and west there were small Christian kingdoms; the most important were Aragon, Castile, León, and Navarre. In 711, however, Muslim army commander Tariq ibn Ziyad led soldiers and settlers from North Africa to conquer southern Spain. It became part of a vast Muslim empire ruled by caliphs in Damascus, Syria.

In 756, Muslim emirs (princes) set up an independent Spanish kingdom based in the trading town of Córdoba. It grew to be one of the largest, richest cities in Europe, with palaces, public baths, fountains, and gardens.

Córdoba also became a great center of scholarship. By 1000, its library contained more than 400,000 books and manuscripts of philosophy, science, mathematics, medicine, history, and poetry.

EMPEROR HENRY IV HUMBLED BY THE POPE

"On 25th day of that month [January 1077], the Emperor Henry IV appeared in front of that castle [Canossa, where the pope was residing] as requested, and, since the castle was surrounded by three rings of walls, he was allowed inside the second ring. His entourage had to wait outside. He stood divested of his royal garments, without the insignia of his dignity, without ornaments of any kind. He was barefoot and fasted from morning to evening in the expectation of the sentence of the Roman pope. He had to do this for a second and a third day. On the fourth day he was allowed to appear before the pope and was told that his excommunication would be repealed under certain conditions."

Lambert of Hersfel, a medieval chronicler

◀ Wonderful stonework and carved plaster in typical Spanish Muslim style decorate the entrance to the Grand Mosque, which still stands at Córdoba, Spain. It was built for scholarly ruler Caliph al-Hakam II in the tenth century.

ABÐ AR-RAHMAN III, RULER OF CÓRÐOBA, (912–961)

A great soldier and administrator, Abd ar-Rahman increased Muslim power in Spain by winning battles against the Christian kings of León and Navarre. He also fought rival Muslims in North Africa and took the title "caliph" to claim power over them. He sent ambassadors to negotiate with German and Byzantine princes. He gave enormous sums of money for magnificent new buildings made and decorated by Muslim and Christian artists.

Many were collected by Caliph al-Hakam II (ruled 961–975); he employed scribes to make copies of important texts by Christian, Jewish, and Muslim scholars from many lands.

Like the rest of Muslim Spain, Córdoba had places of worship for Muslims, Christians, and Jews. Muslim rulers encouraged skilled and learned people from all three faiths to live in Spain and benefit the whole community. Non-Muslims had to pay extra taxes if they wanted to follow their own religion, and Muslim laws ruled community life. Relations between different groups were peaceful on the whole. A brilliant new multicultural civilization developed, blending art, crafts, music, food, technology, and languages from many lands.

Conflict and Collapse

In 975, a fiercely religious new caliph, al-Mansur the Victorious, came to power in Córdoba. He would not tolerate other faiths. He led Muslim armies against Spanish Christian kingdoms, destroyed books and works of art in Córdoba, and drove out non-Muslims. After his death in 1002,

▷ A Christian (*left*) and a Muslim (*right*) enjoy a peaceful game of chess. Chess probably originated in India and was introduced to Europe by Muslims who came to live in Spain.

a civil war developed as his sons battled for power. Spanish Muslims moved away and lived in small, scattered Muslim regions farther south in Spain.

Spanish Christians joined in the fighting, hoping to drive Muslims out of Spain. In 1085, Christian warlord El Cid captured Valencia in southeastern Spain. Then, in 1095 and 1170, southern Spain was invaded by Almoravids and Almohads who were Muslims from North Africa. Christian kings, especially Alfonso I of Portugal and Ferdinand III of Castile and León (now Spain), carried on the fight against Muslim settlers. Alfonso freed Portuguese territory south of Lisbon by 1147, and his grandson, Alfonso III, reconquered all of Portugal from the Muslims by 1249. Ferdinand captured Córdoba in 1236 and Seville in 1248. The last Muslim ruler in the Iberian peninsula, Boabdil of Granada, was expelled by King Ferdinand of León and Queen Isabella of Castile by 1493.

England and France

In medieval England and France, the years from around 1000 to 1300 saw rulers facing new challenges. How could they make their kingdoms bigger and richer? How could they keep hold of

power and pass it on to their sons? How could they make their subjects obey them? Most importantly, what was the best way to rule?

In the fall of 1066, Anglo-Saxon King Harold of England was killed fighting Norman invaders from France. Their leader, Duke William (William the Conqueror), became King William I of England. A new ruling dynasty, the Normans, had arrived.

At first, many Anglo-Saxons protested against Norman rule. William crushed these protests, however, built castles to control the rebels, and gave their land to his followers. Within twenty years, almost all Anglo-Saxon landowners had been replaced by Norman lords, who spoke French and lived in French style. They occupied their lands in return for serving the king as knights, judges, and royal officials. William also appointed a **civil service** that worked directly for him. In 1086, he commissioned the first survey of English land—the Domesday Book—so that he could collect more taxes.

William died in 1087. His descendants were also strong kings. Henry I (ruled 1100–1135) was a tough lawmaker who tried to create a united government for England and the old Norman lands in France. His grandson, Henry II, restored peace in England after years of a civil war that broke out when Henry I's daughter, Matilda, and his nephew, Stephen, both claimed the right to rule. Henry II appointed many of the clergy to help him govern England. He did not want the Church to become too powerful, however, and threaten his authority within his lands. He quarreled dramatically with his chief minister, Archbishop Thomas Becket—a strong supporter of Church power and independence—and ordered his murder in 1170.

◀ Duke William of Normandy makes a rousing speech to his troops as they prepare to invade England in 1066. This scene comes from the Bayeux Tapestry, a massive wall hanging telling the story of William's struggle to become king of England. It was embroidered by women working for a Norman bishop around 1080.

The Rule of Law

Henry II's son John (ruled 1199–1216) was not at all like his father. He lost lands in France, demanded unfair taxes, ignored his subject's rights, attacked powerful nobles—and scandalized many people by his immoral behavior. In 1215, English nobles demanded justice. They forced John to sign a legal document—the Magna Carta (Great Charter). It said that kings must rule fairly, according to the law, and must respect the rights of their people. This set new standards of behavior for all later English monarchs.

a magna Carta Chapter

"No free man shall be seized or imprisoned, or stripped of his rights or possessions, or outlawed or exiled, or deprived of his standing [position] in any other way, nor will we [the king] proceed with force against him, or send others to do so, except by the lawful judgment of his equals or by the law of the land."

Magna Carta 1215 (Clause 39)

Powerful nobles took further measures to control English rulers after Henry III ran up massive debts in 1258. They forced him to consult a royal council before making important decisions. In 1265, they called representatives of towns and the countryside to Parliament for the first time so they could comment on government plans. At first, such representatives were nobles only. After 1295, though, "two knights of the shire (county)"—chosen by shire law courts—and two burgesses (leading citizens) from each town—chosen by fellow citizens—began to attend parliaments. There were no actual elections at this early stage.

Under the watchful eye of councils and parliaments, English kings made many new laws. For example, Edward I (ruled 1272–1307)

△ This copy of the Magna Carta was made for King Henry of England in 1225. The king's royal seal is fixed to the bottom of the document. It consists of a carved image of the king pressed into melted wax and shows that the document is genuine. Seals were used by medieval kings throughout Europe since most of their subjects could not read or write and could not understand written signatures. They could, however, recognize and accept a royal seal.

appointed village constables (patrolling law officers) and local judges called "justices of the peace." He introduced strict new punishments, such as death for stealing sheep, and gave orders for roadside trees to be cut down so that bandits would have fewer places to hide.

Capetian France

In France, the Capetian family came to power after Charlemagne's last ruling descendant, Louis V the Do-Nothing died without an heir. The Capetian family's leader was French nobleman Hugh Capet (ruled 987–996). The Capetians faced rivalry from other French nobles, but they invented a clever way of keeping their family on the throne. Each king named his heir (usually his oldest son) while he was still alive and had him crowned as king. This meant that no one else could claim the right to rule and made rebellion against the heir a very serious crime.

The Capetians set up a strong, centralized government. They also encouraged their subjects to believe that kings could help them. They held special ceremonies, in which kings touched sick people to cure them of "the King's Evil," a form of tuberculosis. (These so-called royal cures were later copied in England.) Kings also paid poets and historians to tell stories about brave or mysterious royal adventures and to write flattering accounts of their reigns.

▼ King Hugh Capet of France (*in blue, second from left*) acknowledges the surrender of rival nobleman Charles of Lorraine in 991. Charles is shown (*far left, in armor*) offering the keys of his castle to the king. Hugh Capet's struggle to strengthen royal authority was greatly helped by Bishop Adelberon of Laon (*pictured in his cathedral, right*), who used trickery to capture Charles of Lorraine and hand him over to the king.

Expanding Frontiers

English and French kings all tried to expand their kingdoms. England's Henry II (ruled 1154–1189) gained land that is now part of southwestern France peacefully through inheritance and by marrying an ambitious heiress, Eleanor of Aquitaine. In 1191, French King Philip II Augustus went to war, winning most of it back from the incompetent English ruler, King John.

Later, French king Philip IV the Fair (ruled 1268–1314) tried bullying the Roman Catholic Church to get land. He imprisoned one pope and forced another to live in France, away from his supporters in Rome. He made the pope ban the Templars (a rich group of warrior monks) and hand their lands over to him. By 1328, large parts of the land that is now modern France belonged to the Capetian family.

In Britain, English kings set out to conquer all the British Isles. From 1169 to 1171, Henry II went to Ireland to help his ally, King Dermot of Leinster. His troops took control of Dermot's kingdom, and English kings for the next eight hundred years claimed the right to rule all of Ireland. (In 1921, most of Ireland—with the exception of the six counties of Northern Ireland—became the Irish Free State, a dominion of Great Britain. Modern Ireland, or Eire, was

▲ A royal prison servant (*in red, right*) bows low as he brings leaders of the Templars (*in black robes*) before King Philip IV of France (*seated, in red*) and Pope Clement IV (*seated, in green*). Philip IV accused the Templars of heresy (false beliefs) and immorality because he was jealous of their wealth and power. In 1307, after the pope banned their organization, many Templars were executed.

made fully independent in 1937, with Northern Ireland still part of the United Kingdom.)

In 1282, Edward I defeated Llwellyn ap Gruffud, the last independent Prince of Wales, and had his head sent to London, where it was displayed on a spiked pole. In 1296, Edward invaded Scotland. Led by patriotic fighters William Wallace and Robert the Bruce, the **Scots** fought back and Edward was killed. Troops sent by his son, Edward II (ruled 1307–1327), were defeated at Bannockburn in 1314. His grandson, Edward III (ruled 1327–1377), was grudgingly forced to admit Scotland's independence in 1328.

CHAPTER 4

Europe and Beyond

ravel in Europe was slow and difficult in medieval times because of bandits and bad, poorly marked roads. Even so, European kingdoms and their rulers were not cut off from other parts of the world. European traders traveled through North Africa and the Middle East. By the thirteenth century, a few were making long overland journeys through Asia as far east as China. They were also in contact with Muslim merchants who sailed across the Indian Ocean to the Spice Islands of Indonesia.

Crusader Kings

Some of the closest—and most uncomfortable—contacts between Europe and elsewhere took place through wars, especially the Crusades. These were wars between Christians and non-Christians. Christians fought against **heretics** in France, and German knights and princes battled against pagan peoples on the shores of the Baltic Sea. The most important of these wars, however, were fought by Christians against Muslims in the Middle East between 1096 and 1493. Christian and Muslim rulers all wanted to control the Holy Land, the area where Jesus Christ lived and died. The city of Jerusalem in the Holy Land was sacred to Christians, Muslims, and Jews. Those calling for Crusades in the Middle East, whether they were popes or rulers, wanted to liberate holy places, such as Jerusalem and other holy sites, from Muslims. They also wanted to defend Christian people living in the Holy Land from Muslim domination.

THE POPE CALLS FOR CRUSADERS

"It is necessary for you to run as quickly as you can to the aid of your brothers living on the eastern shore. . . . I appeal directly to those present. . . . All men going there who die early deaths, whether on the journey by land or sea or while fighting the Muslims, will immediately have their sins forgiven."
Pope Urban II, 1095 [10]

▶ *Above:* Christian leaders of the Crusade meet to discuss battle plans. *Below:* Christian knights charge toward Muslim soldiers and civilians trapped inside the besieged city of Damascus (now in Syria) during the Second Crusade, fought from 1147 to 1149.

◀ King Louis IX of France (*in blue, with crown*) boards a ship to sail to the Holy Land to take part in the Crusades. Although this picture is not drawn to scale, it shows how simple—and crowded—medieval ships could be. Setting sail was dangerous, even in fine weather.

Muslims had ruled the Holy Land since 636, but Jewish and Christian people also had lived there peacefully. Christian pilgrims traveled there to visit holy sites. After about 1000, however, new, less-tolerant Muslim rulers came to power. Muslim warriors, the **Seljuk** Turks, who controlled a large empire from Afghanistan to Baghdad (now Iraq) to Turkey, attacked nearby Christian kingdoms. In 1095, Pope Urban II called on all good Christians to liberate the Holy Land.

For Christian rulers, this call was especially urgent. It was part of their sacred duty to defend all Christians, together with holy places, churches, and monasteries. Many medieval people believed that if a king joined in a Crusade, his presence would give Christian armies extra holy power. If a king led a Crusade, then participation was a moral good rather than a moral evil.

In practical terms, Crusade kings certainly provided encouragement to their troops. Some were also brilliant soldiers. The most famous was King Richard I the Lion-Heart of England (ruled 1189–1199), who fought during the Third Crusade. He led crusaders to win important battles but failed to conquer the holy city of Jerusalem. Like other medieval monarchs, he could be ruthless. After capturing the Muslim city of Acre, he ordered all its citizens to be killed.

French King Louis IX, Saint Louis (ruled 1214–1270), also led armies of crusaders. He commanded the Seventh Crusade but was taken prisoner by Muslim soldiers in the delta region of Egypt after his army was outnumbered and surrounded. He was freed after paying a huge **ransom** and set out on a new Eighth Crusade in 1270. However, he died on the journey, probably of bubonic plague. Louis IX was later made a saint because he fought and died while taking part in a crusade.

From 1099 to 1291, Christians ruled four small states in the Holy Land. They felt proud to be ruling the same territory as David, the ancient Jewish king. At first, they governed these Crusade states in the same way as their European kingdoms. They gave land to lords (Christian knights) who fought in their armies and helped them rule. Soon, however, the Christian rulers began to copy Muslim ways of government, such as holding separate law courts for their Christian, Jewish, and Muslim subjects. In addition, they began to copy the rich, magnificent lifestyle of Muslim rulers.

In the Baltic region, from modern-day Estonia to Poland, German knights also set up new states, which they ruled almost like kings. They encouraged Christian soldiers from Germany to settle in these states and dedicated the northernmost—called Livonia (now Latvia)— to the Virgin Mary, mother of Jesus Christ.

Self-Governing Cities

Kings and princes ruled most of medieval Europe. In Italy, though, large areas of land belonged to independent city-states that ruled themselves. They were known as communes (communities) or republics (states ruled by people), copying the name used by ancient Romans for their city from 509 B.C. to 31 B.C..

City-states were governed by councils whose members came from the wealthiest local families. Some were noblemen, but many were merchants who had grown rich through trade. By law, most were elected; nevertheless, many sons followed their fathers as council members. City-state councils set up law courts, appointed judges, collected taxes, and paid for armies just like kings and princes, but they kept more closely in touch with citizens' thoughts and feelings. If councillors displeased the community, there might be riots, plots, or even murders, and they might find themselves out of power.

The richest Italian cities were ports. They grew wealthy from trading with lands all around the Mediterranean Sea. Italian merchants sailed to ports in Turkey, northern Africa, and the Middle East. There, they met traders from India, Central Asia, and China who had valuable goods, such as silks, gems, medicines, and spices.

AT A MIDDLE EASTERN TRADING TOWN, 1437

"The caravan from Asia arrived . . . it brought so many camels with it that I cannot describe them all. . . . The caravan brings with it all the spices, pearls, precious stones, gold, perfumes, linen cloth, parrots, and Indian cats, together with much else . . . which they spread throughout the world. Around one-half goes to merchants based in Egypt . . . the rest goes to the port of Beirut."
Adapted from *Travels and Adventures 1435–1439*, by Pedro Tarfur

"Queen of the Mediterranean"

Venice, in northeastern Italy, was the richest and most powerful Italian city-state. As a symbol of its close links with the sea, its ruler, called the doge, "married" the waves each year by throwing a wedding ring into them. The doge was chosen from Venice's top families. Once in power, he ruled for life. The first doges controlled the government, army, church, and trade. After 1140, however, they shared their powers with a Great Council. Members, mostly merchants, bankers, and top church officials, tried to stop individual doges from taking too much power—or profit— for themselves. Even so, some doges became extraordinarily rich. For example, in 1268 Doge Ranieri Zeno possessed more than 25,000 lire (about equal to the yearly income of a medium-sized city-state).

Members of the Grand Council often disagreed about policy—especially about plans for war. One group, the "Hawks," wanted to fight rival cities; another group, the "Doves," preferred peace. They argued that fighting wasted money and might make Venice poor.

▶ This Italian manuscript, painted about 1360, shows a representative from the powerful Weavers' Guild in Venice offering a copy of the guild's statutes (rules for members) to Doge Francesco Foscari. The weaver is kneeling as a sign that the guild submits to the doge's authority.

Byzantium

After the western Roman Empire collapsed, Roman civilization continued in the eastern Mediterranean region from what is now Croatia to Turkey. From 330 to 1453, emperors ruled a new empire there known as Byzantium. These Byzantine rulers continued Roman traditions, especially Roman laws.

The Byzantines also saw themselves as champions of Christianity and defenders of Western civilization. They spoke Greek rather than Latin, the Roman language, and their art, architecture, music, and scholarship were shaped by neighboring regions in the Middle East and by ancient Greece. After the schism of 1054 that separated the Christian Church into two parts—Roman Catholic and Eastern Orthodox—they supported the Eastern Orthodox branch of the Christian Church.

The most successful Byzantine emperors, such as Justinian the Great (ruled 527–565), were great lawmakers and administrators as well as generous patrons of art, architecture, and scholarship. Their courts were rich and magnificent but often full of violence and political plotting. They demanded strict obedience from their subjects and had tremendous power over them. They relied on advice from army commanders, magistrates, and often their well-educated wives and mothers. Justinian sent his army to conquer southern Italy, northern Africa, and southern Spain, but the empire could control these lands for only about one hundred years. Besides, these regions were too far away from the

◀ This mosaic, made about 547, portrays Justinian's beautiful, controversial wife, Theodora, dressed in magnificent jewelry of gold, precious stones, and pearls. Before marrying Justinian, Theodora had been a popular actress. As empress, she persuaded him to help women and the poor.

BYZANTINE SYSTEM OF GOVERNMENT

"Limit the powers of governors who become too proud. . . . Don't let any generals who are waging active campaigns have too many resources. Wear them out with constant demands, to keep them busy. . . . Don't let any women join the empire councils. Keep ordinary people away from you. Keep your long-term plans secret."
Advice to Emperor Basil II, from a councillor, c. 970 [12]

rest of the empire, and the Byzantines were faced with Muslim conquests.

Turks and Bulgars

Byzantine emperors also thought it was their duty to defend eastern Europe against attack. They paid for a mighty navy, armed with a secret weapon—deadly "Greek fire"—a chemical mixture that started fires that could not be put out. They also recruited the "Varangian Guard" of top Viking and Russian soldiers.

From about 716 until 1014, Byzantine armies fought against tribes of **Bulgars** who attacked from southern Russia. In 811, Bulgar troops killed Emperor Nicephorus and made his skull into a goblet for their ruler, Khan Krum. In return, Byzantine Emperor Basil II, the Bulgar-Slayer, (ruled 976–1025) blinded thousands of Bulgar prisoners and sent them home, led by one-eyed men, to the Bulgar king, Tsar Samuel, who died of shock.

From 1064 onward, Byzantine rulers faced a powerful new enemy—Muslim Seljuk Turks. Led by Alp Arslan, Lion Hero, (ruled 1063–1072), they invaded from central Asia and defeated the Byzantines at Manzikert (now in Turkey) in 1071. The Byzantine emperor was captured but freed after paying a huge ransom.

In 1299, Seljuk lands were organized into a new empire by Sultan Othman I (ruled

▲ Sultan Othman I founded the Ottoman Empire. In 1299, he gave himself a new title, "emir" (prince), to show his increased power. The empire he founded survived in Turkey and the neighboring lands for more than six hundred years, until 1922.

1299–1326), which was named the **Ottoman** Empire after him. After winning the Battle of Kosovo (now in Serbia) in 1389, Ottoman troops took control of Byzantine lands in what are now Serbia, Greece, Bosnia, Bulgaria, and Albania.

In 1453, Ottoman Sultan Mehmet II (ruled 1451–1481) captured the Byzantine capital, Constantinople. The last Byzantine emperor, Constantine IX, died fighting after bravely defending his city for fifty-four days.

ADVICE TO THE KING OF SERBIA, 1389

"Honored ruler, which Kingdom will you support now? Will you be loyal to the Kingdom of Heaven, or the kingdoms of this world? If you choose the earthly kingdom, get your horses ready for war! Let all your knights sharpen their swords, and rush side-by-side against the Turks. . . . But if you choose the Kingdom of Heaven, then build a church on the Field of Kosovo."
Translation adapted by the author

CHAPTER 5

Rival Rulers

 or centuries, European kings married only women from royal or noble families. This tradition was a way of preserving their special, godlike status, getting more land, and sometimes, making peace. On the other hand, many royal marriages led to serious problems. By about 1300, European royal families were very closely related, which meant that princes from more than one country might claim to be rightful ruler of the same kingdom.

The Hundred Years War

From 1337 to 1453, English and French rulers both claimed to rule lands in France. This dispute led to a series of battles known as the Hundred Years War. It began after French King Charles IV (ruled 1322–1328) died without a son to follow him. French nobles decided to ask Charles's cousin, Philip VI, to be king. English King Edward III (ruled 1327–1377), however, also claimed the French throne. His mother was the sister of the dead King Charles IV. The English, who did not like her, called her the "She-Wolf of France."

Edward III was a famous warrior—remarkably tough and brave. He became king at fourteen years old, after his father, Edward II, was murdered in a plot by his wife and her lover. To show he was in charge, and although only seventeen, Edward then plotted against his mother and her lover; he had the lover executed, then took over power. Edward III was also devoted to **chivalry**, a romantic code of good conduct for warriors. He founded the Order of the Garter, an exclusive brotherhood of knights. It was a great honor to be invited to join.

At first, the Hundred Years War went well for England. Edward won major battles at sea (Sluys, 1340) and on land (Crécy, 1346). Then English and French kings both ran out of money and had to agree to a truce. Fighting began again in 1355, led by Edward's son, also called Edward, the glamorous Black Prince. (He was so called because he wore eye-catching black armor decorated with ostrich plumes.) In 1356, the Black Prince won the Battle of Poitiers and captured the new French king John II. John was set free after the Treaty of Bretigny in 1360, but he had to leave his second son, the duke of Anjou, as a hostage in his place. The duke escaped from prison in 1363, after breaking his parole, or promise—a most dishonorable act. So King John II very chivalrously returned to prison in his place, fell ill there, and died in 1364. In 1376, at age forty-six, Edward the Black Prince died a year before his father, old King Edward III.

The new king of England, Richard II, was the Black Prince's son, but he was only ten years old. In 1380, another child, Charles VI, became king of France at twelve years old. This was a chance for powerful nobles to take over. In England, Edward III's fourth son, John of Gaunt, ran the

Younger Son

Proud, rich, clever and ambitious, John of Gaunt wanted to be a king. He claimed the throne of Castile in Spain after marrying a Spanish princess but failed to win the kingdom by fighting. Gaunt also tried to help his sons win power. His oldest son became king of England, as Henry IV in 1399, after persuading Richard II to abdicate (give up ruling). Gaunt's grandson, Henry V, also became king and was one of England's most famous heroes.

country. In 1396, Gaunt arranged a marriage between Richard II and Charles VI's daughter. This alliance brought peace between England and France for almost twenty years. In 1413, though, a new, warlike English king came to power.

Henry V, king of England (ruled 1413–1422), was determined, ambitious, well-educated, and musical. He believed he was God's deputy on Earth and crushed religious and political protests.

⚑ King John II of France (*on horseback*) surrenders to Edward the Black Prince (*right, in black armor*) at the Battle of Poitiers, fought in France in 1356. Also shown are the powerful English longbows that killed many French knights as well as brutal hand-to-hand fighting.

A brilliant military commander, he dedicated himself to winning back land in France. He defeated the French at Agincourt in 1415, then conquered Normandy. The French were forced to make peace, and Henry married a French princess to demonstrate that he was ruler of France. While Henry V claimed to be king of France, he never had any real power. Henry died two years later from dysentery in 1422 and left a son, King Henry VI, who was just one year old.

▲ King Henry V of England is portrayed in the clothes, jewels—and hairstyle—of a fashionable young English nobleman. Henry's youth, strength, and fighting spirit revived English hopes of winning the Hundred Years War. These hopes disappeared when he died young, leaving a baby as the next king.

French armies seized their chance and fought back. They were helped by a young French girl, Joan of Arc. She claimed to hear heavenly voices telling her to save France. French prince Charles

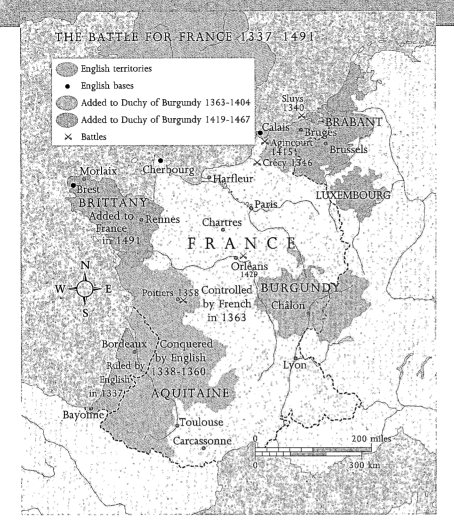

THE BATTLE FOR FRANCE 1337–1491

English territories

● English bases

Added to Duchy of Burgundy 1363-1404

Added to Duchy of Burgundy 1419-1467

✕ Battles

Sluys 1340
Calais ● Bruges
BRABANT
Agincourt 1415
Brussels
Morlaix   Cherbourg
Harfleur
✕ Crécy 1346
Brest
BRITTANY
Added to France in 1491
Rennes   Chartres
Paris
LUXEMBOURG
F R A N C E
N
W—E
S
Orléans 1429
Poitiers 1358 Controlled by French in 1363
BURGUNDY
Châlon
Bordeaux Conquered by English 1338-1360
Ruled by English in 1337
Lyon
AQUITAINE
Bayonne
Toulouse
Carcassonne
0   200 miles
0   300 km

◁ At the start of the Hundred Years War, English King Edward III and French King Philip VI both claimed the right to be king of France. Edward III controlled only a small area of the country, however, while Philip ruled most of the land. In the early years of the war, Edward's army conquered large territories in southwestern France. The French fought back, however, and by 1453, England had lost all its French lands except a small area around the northern seaport of Calais. In the war's later years, English troops were helped by the dukes of Burgundy—rich, ambitious, art-loving rulers of a powerful, fast-growing state on the northeastern borders of France. In 1477, Duke Charles the Bold of Burgundy was killed fighting and left no son to reign after him. The French king seized half his lands and added them to his kingdom. The remaining Burgundy lands passed to the Hapsburg dynasty, rulers of the Holy Roman Empire. The Duchy of Brittany remained independent from English and French kings throughout the Hundred Years War. It was taken over by France in 1491.

(son of Charles VI) realized Joan could inspire his soldiers. He let her dress in armor and lead his army in battle. They won, and he became king as Charles VII the Victorious (ruled 1422–1461). By 1453 when the war ended, England had lost almost all its land in France.

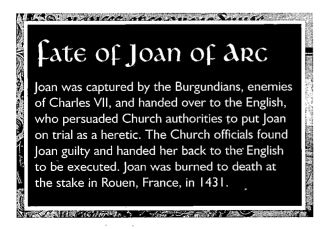

fate of Joan of Arc

Joan was captured by the Burgundians, enemies of Charles VII, and handed over to the English, who persuaded Church authorities to put Joan on trial as a heretic. The Church officials found Joan guilty and handed her back to the English to be executed. Joan was burned to death at the stake in Rouen, France, in 1431.

People Power

To pay for armies and wars, medieval kings needed money. In England and France, the Hundred Years War was so expensive that kings invented new taxes. In England, these were poll taxes, or per-head taxes, paid by all adults, even the poor, and considered highly unfair. At that time, England—like France and other parts of Europe—was facing serious economic problems caused by famine and disease. From 1346 to 1353, Europe was devastated by an epidemic of bubonic plague, called the Black Death by later historians. Up to one-half of the population died. (There were smaller outbreaks of plague during the rest of the Middle Ages.) To ordinary people, the taxes seemed unbearable. They were also angered by new laws, which stopped them from getting higher wages. In addition, they demanded

△ Wat Tyler, leader of the English Peasants' Revolt, is killed by the Lord Mayor of London (*far left*) in 1381. Teenage King Richard II (*on horseback, with crown*) looks on. Before marching on London, Tyler had led mobs of angry peasants to capture the city of Canterbury in southeastern England.

freedom for all men and women who were still classified as **serfs** by the law.

In England, France, and Flanders (now Belgium), ordinary people took part in violent protests and attacked royal advisors, such as John of Gaunt. The first revolt was in Flanders, from 1323 to 1328. Peasants refused to pay taxes and fought against royal armies. In 1358, French peasants protested against the damage caused by armies fighting over their land. In the violence, called the Jacquerie, that followed, more than twenty thousand peasants were killed by soldiers loyal to the French king.

In 1381, mobs of laborers marched on London and demanded to see the king. Richard II, who was only fourteen, was in real danger. His troops could not control London nor defeat the angry protesters. So he tried friendship—and trickery. He rode out to speak to the mob and promised to abolish serfdom. Many laborers went home, satisfied, but then the lord mayor of London stabbed the mob leader and killed him. The laborers scattered, fearing for their lives. King Richard canceled his promise, but the protesters had given kings a clear warning. If kings angered their people, they might lose their thrones.

Conflicts with Nobles

Royal marriages meant that there were many European noble families descended from sons or daughters of kings. They owned large estates, kept private armies, and acted as royal advisers. They had strong family ties with ruling monarchs and often wanted a share of their power. Throughout the Middle Ages, many kings had real problems keeping these noble families under control.

For example, in England after 1400, weak kings and strong nobles led to years of civil war. It began during the reign of King Henry VI of England (ruled 1422–1471). Henry was a tragic character. Son of hero-king Henry V, he was gentle and peace loving. For most of his life, he suffered from mental illness. He was so religious that some people called him a saint. His reign, however, was a disaster. He could not provide leadership in the war with France, good government at home, or stop ambitious nobles from plotting to take power away from him.

In 1453, Henry VI became too ill to rule. His cousin, Richard, ran the government for him. Like Henry, Richard was descended from King Edward III, but he belonged to a different branch of the royal family. King Henry was the duke of Lancaster. Richard was duke of York.

Two years later, Henry recovered from his illness and wanted to rule once more as king. Richard, however, refused to hand over power, and their respective supporters—the Lancastrians and the Yorkists—began to fight. For the next twenty years, there was bloodshed and confusion. This period was called the Wars of the Roses because Yorkists and Lancastrians both had roses as their family emblems.

The Wars of the Roses ended when a distant member of the Lancastrian family became king in 1485. His name was Henry Tudor, and he was descended from John of Gaunt. He ruled as Henry VII until 1509. To make peace, he married a Yorkist princess, daughter of Edward IV. Together, they founded the Tudors, a new royal family. Tudor monarchs ruled England and Wales for more than one hundred years.

the Wars of the Roses

1449–1451 Parliament complains about King Henry VI (Duke of Lancaster) and his advisers.

1453 King Henry VI becomes ill.

1453 Duke Richard (of York) rules.

1460 Duke Richard is murdered.

1461 King Henry VI turned off the throne by Yorkists; Duke Richard's son becomes King Edward IV (as Yorkist).

1471 Henry VI is murdered.

1483 Edward IV dies; Edward IV's son becomes King Edward V (Yorkist); King Edward V and his brother are probably murdered by their uncle, Richard (Yorkist); Richard becomes King Richard III.

1485 Richard III killed in battle by Lancastrians; Henry Tudor (Lancastrian) becomes King Henry VII.

a new europe

n 1500, at the end of the Middle Ages, kings and princes still ruled most of Europe. Eastern Europe had become part of the Muslim Ottoman Empire, but Muslim caliphs no longer ruled southern Spain. The frontiers of most kingdoms were more firmly fixed than they had been in 500 or 1000. The peoples of most kingdoms were more united and more tightly under their rulers' control. Christian Church leaders, whether they were Roman Catholic or Eastern Orthodox, still taught that rulers were sent by God. Furthermore, they still told kings and princes that ruling was a sacred duty.

New Limits

In spite of this, European kings in 1500 did not have as much power as earlier monarchs had. Although some still did win their thrones by fighting, most had to obey strict laws governing inheritance of land. The Church oversaw these laws, and it was a sin to disobey them. Many monarchs had to consult councils or parliaments before making important decisions or raising taxes. When running governments, they had to negotiate with powerful noble landowners. While these landowners were sometimes close royal relatives, they still all had political aims and ambitions of their own.

the Medici family in florence, 1434–1494
- Cosimo de Medici the Elder (ruled 1434–1464): Owned a bank; used his wealth to win power and to improve the city. Paid for many works of art and buildings in new Renaissance style. Set up Europe's first public library. Encouraged scholars and philosophers.
- Piero de Medici (ruled 1464–1468): Skilled politician; died young.
- Lorenzo de Medici the Magnificent (ruled 1469–1492): Great patron of literature and the arts. Made Florence the leading state in Italy.
- Piero de Medici the Unfortunate (ruled 1492–1494): Proud and willful. Angered people of Florence. Fought against French, who took control. Banished from city and died fighting.

◀ Lorenzo de Medici, ruler of Florence, Italy, is portrayed as a king from a Bible story in a painting on the walls of a splendid new chapel he commissioned and funded. Images like this show how medieval rulers hoped to be honored during their lifetime and remembered after their death.

◀ Prince Henry the Navigator of Portugal was the third son of King John I of Portugal. He took a keen interest in travel and exploration during the fifteenth century. He set up a college for navigators and funded many voyages to explore the western coast of Africa. Information gathered on these voyages helped many later explorers, including Christopher Columbus.

In addition, monarchs had to deal with some new ruling families who were not royal at all. The most powerful of these were in Italy, where merchants and bankers ruled rich city-states. Their wealth allowed them to pay for professional armies and to build magnificent palaces, churches, council chambers, and other public buildings as signs of their prestige and power. They were strong enough to challenge other European leaders, especially the Holy Roman Emperor and the pope.

New Ideas

Late medieval rulers also faced challenges from new ideas. After peasant protests and revolts in the 1300s, some scholars began to suggest that kings needed the agreement of their subjects to rule. After kings and princes in Spain and Portugal financed voyages of exploration in the 1400s, Europe came into contact with a wide "new world" in West Africa, the Americas, and Southeast Asia.

Isabella and Columbus

Isabella of Castile (ruled 1474–1504) won the right to inherit her father's kingdom in northern Spain. She was helped by her mother who gave her political backing rather than forcing her to marry some prince or noble. Isabella also demanded to choose her own husband—Ferdinand of Aragon—at a time when most royal marriages were arranged. With him, she drove Muslims and Jews out of Spain. At the same time, at home, she was forward looking and interested in new ideas. She founded new schools, encouraged artists and scholars, and paid for Christopher Columbus's first voyage to America.

C. 370-600
"Barbarian" invaders attack the Roman Empire. Goth and Visigoth kings rule in Italy, France, and Spain.

395
The Roman Empire is divided into eastern and western halves.

476
The last Roman emperor is forced to flee from Rome and the western Roman Empire collapses.

527-565
Justinian the Great makes new laws based on Roman ideas to rule Byzantine Empire.

568
Lombard kings conquer northern Italy.

C. 700
Anglo-Saxon kings rule the seven kingdoms in England.

711
Muslim leader Tariq ibn Ziyad conquers southern Spain.

800
Charlemagne, king of the Franks, is crowned Holy Roman Emperor.

C. 800-C. 1100
Viking warlords (later kings) lead raids in many parts of Europe.

843
Kenneth MacAlpine becomes first king of a united Scottish kingdom.

844
Rhodri Mawr becomes first king to rule almost all of Wales.

871-899
Alfred the Great is king of Wessex, England.

886-954
Danelaw, the Viking kingdom, rules in northeastern England.

912-961
Abd ar-Rahman III becomes ruler of Córdoba.

924-939
Athelstan is first king to rule all England.

962
Otto I the Great of Germany is crowned emperor by the pope.

997
Stephen becomes first king of Hungary; he is made a saint in 1083.

1016-1035
Viking King Canute rules empire in Scandinavia and Britain.

1075-1122
Intense quarrels break out between Holy Roman Emperors and popes.

1066
Normans win Battle of Hastings in England. William the Conqueror rules England.

1071
Seljuk Turks defeat Byzantines at the Battle of Manzikert.

1096-1291
Crusader kings invade Muslim lands and set up Crusader states.

1152-1190
Holy Roman Emperor Frederick I Barbarossa takes control of vast new lands.

1169-1171
Henry II of England sends soldiers to Ireland.

C. 1200
Republican city-states in Italy grow powerful through overseas trade.

1215
Nobles force King John of England to sign Magna Carta.

1236
King Ferdinand III captures Córdoba in present-day Spain from Muslims.

1265
Representatives of towns and countryside are called to English Parliament for first time.

1282
Edward I of England conquers Wales; fourteen years later, he invades Scotland.

1299
Othman I becomes first Ottoman emperor in Turkey.

1328
French royal family takes control of most of the land today known as France.

1337-1453
French and English kings claim to rule the same land during the Hundred Years War.

1340, 1346, 1356
English King Edward III and his son, the Black Prince, win famous victories against France.

1381
Peasant revolt breaks out in England.

1389
After the Battle of Kosovo in Serbia, Ottoman Sultan Mehmet I conquers the Balkans region of Europe.

1415
King Henry V of England wins Battle of Agincourt; England defeats France.

1429
French King Charles VII, helped by Joan of Arc, defeats English at Orléans, France.

1434-1494
Medici family rules city-state of Florence in Italy.

1453
Ottoman Sultan Mehmet II captures Constantinople. The last Byzantine emperor dies.

1455-1485
The Wars of the Roses is fought between rival nobles wanting to be king in England.

1485
King Henry VII founds Tudor ruling dynasty in England and Wales.

1492
Queen Isabella and King Ferdinand drive Muslims and Jews from Spain.

Source References:

[1] C. Warren Hollister, *Medieval Europe: A Short History*, Wiley, 1964, p. 1.

[2] R. McKitterick (ed.), *Medieval World*, Times Books, 2003, p. 27.

[3] The Anglo-Saxon Chronicle was originally compiled on the orders of Alfred the Great in A.D. 890. It was added to by generations of anonymous scribes until the middle of the twelfth century.

[4] R. McKitterick (ed.), *see above*, p. 27.

[5] Henry of Huntingdon. D. Danziger and J. Gillingham, *1215, The Year of Magna Carta*, Hodder and Stoughton, 2003, p. 169.

[6] Constantine VII. R. McKitterick (ed.), *see above*, p. 73.

[7] Adapted from E.R.A. Sewter (ed.), *The Alexiad of Anna Comnena*, Penguin Classics, 1969, pp. 118–119.

[8] H. Leyser, *Medieval Women*, Phoenix, 1996, p. 81.

[9] Lambert of Hersfel. Quoted in F. Heer (ed.), *The Fires of Faith*, Wiedenfeld and Nicolson, 1970, p. 121.

[10] Pope Urban II. Adapted from J. Riley Smith, *The Crusades, Idea and Reality, 1095–1174*, Edward Arnold, 1981.

[11] Original quoted in Peter Spufford, *Power and Profit, The Merchant in Medieval Europe*, Thames and Hudson, 2002, p. 346.

[12] Adapted from E.R.A. Sewter (ed.), *Fourteen Byzantine Rulers*, 1966, p. 43.

[13] Quoted in R. Marks and P. Williamson, *Gothic—Art for England, 1400-1547*, Victoria and Albert Museum, 2003, p. 36.

Angles People from Germany and Denmark who settled in Britain from about A.D. 40

barbarian An ancient Greek word used by Romans and later by Europeans to describe foreigners. It suggests that foreigners are wild, brutal, and savage.

brocade Cloth—usually silk—with a rich woven pattern of curving lines, fruits, and flowers originally made in the Middle East, later copied in Europe

Bulgars Turkish-speaking tribes from lands north of the Black Sea who settled in eastern Europe from about A.D. 700.

Byzantium A powerful empire in eastern Europe and Turkey from A.D. 395 to 1453

caliph Muslim ruler; successor of the prophet Muhammad as religious and political leader of the Muslim community. In the early years of Muslim power, there was only one caliph. After about A.D. 900, several rival Muslim leaders claimed the title.

caravans Travelers who group together to help each other, usually in a hostile region, such as a desert

Celtic Describes a European civilization powerful from about 800 B.C. to A.D. 100. Celtic traditions continued in far western Europe—Scotland, Ireland, Wales, Isle of Man, and Brittany (in France)—for about another nine hundred years.

chivalry Polite, honorable behavior by noble knights. Chivalrous knights were supposed to be loyal to their king, gallant toward women, and generous to the poor and weak, and to defend the Christian Church.

chronicles Written descriptions of important events, mostly compiled by medieval monks

civil service An appointed branch of government that helps a ruler administer a realm

coat of arms Badge or symbol originally worn by lords, knights, and their soldiers to identify themselves in battle. It became a sign of high rank.

coronation Holy ceremony in which a ruler is given a crown and blessed by Church leaders

Crusades Wars fought between Christians and Muslims or between Christians and pagans or heretics

Danegeld Money paid by English kings to Viking kings and warlords, so that Viking warriors would not raid their land

Danelaw Land in northeastern England ruled by Vikings

divine right The right to rule given by God

doge A leader in certain Italian city–states, such as Venice

duchy A territory or domain ruled by a duke

estates Large areas of land owned by one family

excommunicated Banned from all important Christian Church services. This caused practical problems, such as being unable to inherit land. It also made Christians fear that they would die in a state of sinfulness and be punished after death in hell.

feuds Long-running quarrels between families or other close groups

Franks People who migrated to settle in France from about A.D. 300

heretics Word used by Christian leaders to describe religious dissidents—men or women whose religious beliefs differed from the official teachings of the Christian Church

inheritance Describes process in which land, goods, money, or a kingdom is passed from parents to children or other close relatives at death

interdict A Church punishment, often used against monarchs who quarrelled with Church leaders, banning all baptisms, marriages, and burials

knights Well-trained warriors, mostly from high-ranking families; they fought as officers in medieval kings' armies and often helped monarchs run civilian government as well.

Lombards "Barbarian" tribes that invaded northern Italy in A.D. 568

Magyars Nomadic people from Russia who migrated to Hungary about A.D. 900

manuscripts Documents written by hand

medieval A word that relates to and describes the Middle Ages

mosaic Describes images made from little pieces of colored glass, pottery, or stone

Ottoman Muslim empire in the Middle East, powerful from 1299 to the early twentieth century

pagans Word used by Christians and Muslims to describe people who did not share their faith

parliaments Conferences to discuss public affairs, or the organization of political groups to form a government

Pict A Celtic people who lived in eastern Scotland

ransom Money paid to set prisoners free or to release a kidnapped victim

Roman Empire The people and lands that belonged to ancient Rome, consisting of most of southern Europe and northern Africa from Britain to the Middle East

Saxons People who lived in southern Germany and migrated to England after about A.D. 400

Scots Celtic people who lived in western Scotland and Ireland

Seljuks Nomadic Turkish-speaking tribes that invaded the Middle East and settled there from about A.D. 1000 onward

serfs Peasants who belonged to a rich or noble landowner and were not free to move, leave his land, or even get married without his permission. They also had to work for him on his farmland or pay him rent money instead.

status Position in society

Vikings Raiders, traders, and settlers from Scandinavia, powerful from about A.D. 800 to 1100

Books:

Bartlett, Robert. *Medieval Panorama*. New York: Thames and Hudson, 2001.
Deary, Terry. *Cruel Kings and Mean Queens*. New York: Scholastic, 1995.
Evans, Joan. *The Flowering of the Middle Ages*. New York: Thames and Hudson, 1969.
Langley, Andrew. *Medieval Life* (Eyewitness Books). New York: DK Publishing, 2002.
Leon,Vicki. *Outrageous Women of the Middle Ages*. New York: John Wiley, 1998.
Loyn, Henry R. (ed.). *The Middle Ages, A Concise Encyclopedia*. New York: Thames and Hudson, 1991.
Macdonald, Fiona. *Women in Medieval Times*. Lincolnwood, IL: Peter Bedrick Books, 2000.

Web Sites:

Explore the Middle Ages
www.learner.org/exhibits/middleages
*Find out how medieval monarchs—and their subjects—lived. What did
medieval people have for breakfast? What sports did they play? What clothes
did they wear?*

Introducing the Middle Ages
www.mrdowling.com/703middleages.html
*Search this site for short, simple articles on the Vikings, the Crusades, barbarian invasions, and
much more.*

Kidsclick!
www.kidsclick.org/topgeog.html
Find links to Web sites on history and biography, specially chosen for children by librarians.

Kings, Knights, and Armies
www.metmuseum.org/explore/knights/home.html
*This is a site for older readers and adults. Most medieval kings were warriors, who led armies of knights
and foot soldiers. Find out about how they fought and about their weapons and armor.*

Show Me!
www.show.me.uk/topic/topic.html
*This Web site provides links to sites for children run by museums. Try the sections on Anglo-Saxons
and Vikings.*

Sir Clisto Seversword's Tome of Adventure & Knowledge
www.sirclisto.com/clisto2.html
This fun site allows younger readers to find out loads of information about the Middle Ages.

Treasures of an Anglo-Saxon King
www.thebritishmuseum.ac.uk
*This enormous site contains lots about the Anglo-Saxon—and hidden
treasures from an Anglo-Saxon king's burial. Connect to the museum's
home page, then go to "Children's Compass," then "Curriculum Search,"
then "Subjects," then "History," then "KS2 Anglo-Saxon England," and
"KS2 Sutton Hoo."*